WOMAN, GO BE: SELF LOVE WORKBOOK

ISBN: 979-8-9856190-4-1

For more information, visit iamlatoyanicole.com

This book belongs to:

_____

Welcome to the Woman, Go Be Workbook - your personal guide empowering you to move from feelings of being stuck to a place of growth and fulfillment. This workbook is a space where you can explore, reflect, and take intentional steps towards creating a healthier version of yourself.

Now, take a deep breath, exhale, and be honest with yourself as you embrace the essence of the woman you were meant to become. As you continue to move forward, every step you take brings you closer to a life filled with genuine happiness and healing.

Speaking joy, wholeness, and a transformation in your life.

xo,

Latoya Nicole

Why is healing important?

Healing allows us to recover and restore our well-being, whether it's physical, emotional, or spiritual. Healing is a natural process that helps us recover from illnesses, injuries, or traumas, and it promotes the body's ability to regain balance and function at its best self.

Physically, healing plays a vital role in improving our overall quality of life. When we are in good health, we have the energy and ability to engage in daily activities, pursue our goals, and enjoy life as a whole.

Emotionally, healing is crucial for our mental health and overall happiness. It enables us to work through and overcome emotional wounds, such as grief or relationship difficulties and gives us the confidence needed to get unstuck and finally move forward. By addressing and resolving these issues, we can experience personal growth and develop healthier ways to cope.

Spiritually, healing can equip you to love and show compassion to others who are in need of healing whether through prayer or support. It is also the stepping stone to being able to walk into your purpose of who God has called you to be. Remember the woman in the bible that had the issue of blood - she not only experienced a physical healing where the blood issue was stopped but she also experienced an emotional and spiritual healing, as she was no longer in distress and separated from those she loved or from her relationship with Jesus. After she touched him, Jesus told her your faith has made you whole.

Healing bring wholeness. Through the healing process, we can gain a deeper understanding of ourselves and make intentional changes to live a more fulfilling life.

With that said, healing can sometimes bring up fear because we may have to confront painful memories, face our vulnerabilities, or step into the unknown. The first step in healing is being honest with yourself. If fear is coming up in your life right now write a paragraph or a series of bullet points articulating your fear in detail.

Over time, you can revisit this to track your progress, identify patterns, and celebrate your growth and achievements.

What am I afraid of?

Where do I believe that fear comes from?

What specifically triggers this fear?

How does fear impact my daily life or decision-making?

How does fear hold me back or prevent personal growth?

Find a scripture that speaks against each fear.

Break down the fear into smaller, manageable steps, and gradually work your way up to facing the fear head-on.

If you have a fear of public speaking - Here's an example of breaking down that fear into smaller steps:

1. Start by practicing alone: Begin by rehearsing your speech or presentation in the privacy of your own space. Practice speaking aloud, even if it's just in front of a mirror or recording yourself.
2. Take the next step and share your speech with a friend or family member. Deliver it to them in a comfortable and supportive environment. Their feedback and encouragement can boost your confidence.
3. Volunteer for small speaking engagements: These smaller speaking engagements can help you build your skills and experience.
4. Seek opportunities for larger speaking engagements: As you gain more confidence and experience, start seeking opportunities for larger speaking engagements. This could include conferences, panel discussions, or seminars. Remember to keep practicing and refining your skills along the way.

By breaking down the fear of public speaking into smaller, manageable steps, and gradually working your way up to larger speaking engagements, you can build confidence, overcome anxiety, and ultimately conquer your fear so that it no longer overshadows you when you get ready to do it.

Use this next section to break down each fear into smaller steps:

Fear #1

Fear #2

Fear #3

Fear #4

Keep going,
you're doing great!

Fear #5

Fear #6

Fear #7

Fear #8

Fear #9

Creative Activity: "Fearless Collage"

This activity provides an outlet for self-expression and inspiration during your journey of overcoming fear.

Instructions:

1. Gather magazines, newspapers and glue. Cut out images and words that resonate with you and reflect your aspirations.
2. Create a collage that represents your journey in overcoming fear.
3. Arrange and glue the cutouts onto the blank page in a way that feels meaningful and empowering.
4. Reflect on each element you include and how it relates to your fear and the process of working through it.
5. Get creative using colors, patterns, and additional drawings or symbols to enhance the collage.
6. Once completed, title your collage and write a brief description of what it represents to you.

Use this space to create your collage

Use this space to revisit your collage later, adding notes about your progress and any insights gained.

Extra free space

Extra free space

I slept on myself way too long.
I'm woke now.

The Awakening

Reflecting on Your Past

Take some time to reflect on your past experiences and the significant moments that have shaped you into the person you are today. Engaging in this exercise will allow you to gain insights into your journey and understand how it has influenced your beliefs, values, and perspectives.
Find a quiet space, and let the memories flow. Use photos to help you reflect.

Reflections:

Think about a difficult time or challenge in your life that was hard for you to cope with. How did you handle the situation at the time?

What was the most difficult aspect of that situation?

How did you cope?

How did you overcome the situation?

Did you look to anyone for outside support? If so, who was that person?

What skills helped you deal with the situation?

What is some advice you would give to your current self today if you were in a similar situation?

Write about three pivotal moments or experiences from your past that have had a profound impact on your life.

#1

#2

#3

How did they shape your beliefs, values, or self-perception?

What lessons did you learn from those experiences, and how have they contributed to your personal growth?

#1

#2

#3

Additional space:

Exploring Your Values

Understanding your values is essential for aligning your life with what truly matters to you. In this section, you'll explore your core values. By identifying your values and where you are now, you gain insight to guide your decision-making, relationships, and overall fulfillment.

List five values that are most important to you.

Consider what brings you a sense of fulfillment, what qualities you admire in others, and the principles you consider most. Reflect on how you can live in alignment with these values and integrate them more into your daily life.

What are your strengths?

Make a list of your top five strengths. Reflect on the skills, talents, or qualities that come naturally to you and set you apart. Consider how you can leverage these strengths in various areas of your life, such as your relationships, in business, or personally. Embrace your strengths as gifts that contribute to your overall well-being and success.

What are your spiritual gifts?

Understanding your current position allows you to evaluate whether you are on the right path or if adjustments are needed.

Gratitude plays an important role in helping you figure out where you are in life. When you practice gratitude, you cultivate a mindset of appreciation and focus on the positive aspects of your life. Here's how gratitude can assist you in gaining clarity about your present situation:

1. Shifts your focus from lack to abundance: Instead of dwelling on what's missing or what hasn't gone as planned, gratitude helps you recognize and appreciate the blessings, opportunities, and achievements in your life.
2. Enhances self-awareness: Expressing gratitude requires reflection and introspection. When you intentionally acknowledge the things you are grateful for, you become more aware of your values, priorities, and desires. This can help you understand what truly matters to you and guide you in aligning your actions and decisions.
3. Provides perspective: Gratitude allows you to step back and gain a broader perspective. It helps you recognize various aspects of your life, such as relationships, achievements, personal growth, and experiences.

GRATITUDE REFLECTION

WRITE WHAT YOU ARE GRATEFUL FOR TODAY:

_____

_____

_____

_____

DESCRIBE WHAT YOU LOVE ABOUT YOURSELF:

_____

_____

_____

DESCRIBE WHAT YOU ARE EXCITED ABOUT:

_____

_____

HOW DO YOU FEEL TODAY?

DRAW YOUR MOOD ON HER FACE.

FAVORITE QUOTE

K E Y S

- [ ] BLESSED
- [ ] GOOD
- [ ] PRODUCTIVE
- [ ] AVERAGE
- [ ] RELAXED
- [ ] EXHAUSTED
- [ ] DEPRESSED
- [ ] BORED
- [ ] SICK

NOTES

What do you need to heal from?

Write down three goals you have for your healing journey. What do you want to achieve? How do you want to feel?

Additional space:

Additional space:

Additional space:

Additional space:

Take time
to heal,
to grow,
to become.

Self Love and Healing

What is self love?

In this section, we're going on a transformative journey of healing, self-love, and personal growth. This lesson will empower you to explore techniques and exercises that will help you confront and release the pain, traumas, or negative experiences that may have held you back. By creating a space for healing you allow yourself to move forward with a renewed sense of wholeness and freedom.

Self Love Questions

What do I need in order to feel safe?

How important is my own happiness?

In what ways do I show love for myself?

Self Love Journey

I feel loved when?

I feel confident when?

I feel blessed when?

I feel proud when?

Name something good that happened to you today

Self Improvement

My Good Qualities

Qualities I want to keep or add

Yass sis! Those qualities about you are looking good!

BUT, NOW....

list those *not so good* qualities that you know for sure about yourself or that someone you trust has said about you.

Self Improvement

Not so good qualities

Qualities you want to change

SELF CARE
CHECKLIST

- [ ] Stay hydrated
- [ ] Read a new book
- [ ] spend time outside
- [ ] Do something kind
- [ ] Try a new exercise
- [ ] listen to music

Self Improvement

New Skills to Learn

Self-care Affirmations

1	I am worthy of love, care, and kindness.
2	I prioritize my well-being and make time for self-care.
3	I am capable of great things.
4	I am allowed to make mistakes and learn from them.
5	My needs and boundaries are valid and deserving of respect.
6	I am allowed to put myself first.
7	I am allowed to take breaks when I need them.
8	I am allowed to say no.
9	I am allowed to be assertive.
10	I embrace self-compassion and release judgment towards myself.

Self-care Affirmations

1	
2	
3	
4	
5	
6	
7	
8	
9	
10	

The Power of Mindfulness

Mindfulness is the art of being fully present. In this section, we will explore mindfulness techniques that will help you cultivate awareness, reduce stress, and experience a greater sense of peace and clarity. By practicing mindfulness, you can let go of worries about the past or future and find a deeper connection with yourself and the world around you.

CALM YOURSELF WITH A
5 FINGER BREATHING
EXERCISE

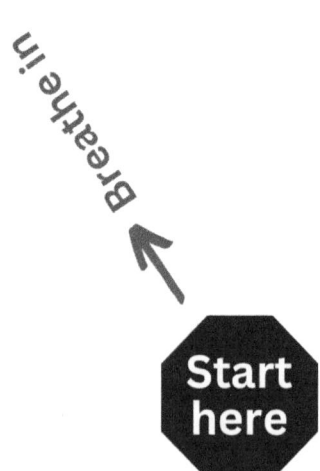

Breathe in

Start here

Slowly trace the outside of your hand, breathing in when you
trace up a finger and breathing out when you trace down.

Feeling Creative?
Draw here.

Feeling Creative?
Color this.

Happiness starts from the inside.

What brings you the most joy?

Explore your purpose, hobbies, and interests. By uncovering what truly makes you happy, you can infuse your life with more meaning and fulfillment. Allow yourself to think about activities that bring you joy and explore new areas that pique your curiosity.

Create a list of activities or interests that excite you. It can be something you already enjoy or new hobbies you'd like to explore. Consider activities that make you lose track of time or bring a smile to your face.

For the next month start incorporating these into your weekly plans to experience more fulfillment and to commit to doing more things that you love doing.

Interests

ACTIVITIES

WEEKLY PLANNER

MONTH :

WEEK :

MONDAY

- [ ] _____
- [ ] _____
- [ ] _____
- [ ] _____

TUESDAY

- [ ] _____
- [ ] _____
- [ ] _____
- [ ] _____

WEDNESDAY

- [ ] _____
- [ ] _____
- [ ] _____
- [ ] _____

THURSDAY

- [ ] _____
- [ ] _____
- [ ] _____
- [ ] _____

FRIDAY

- [ ] _____
- [ ] _____
- [ ] _____
- [ ] _____

SATURDAY

- [ ] _____
- [ ] _____
- [ ] _____
- [ ] _____

SUNDAY

- [ ] _____
- [ ] _____
- [ ] _____
- [ ] _____

NOTE :

WEEKLY PLANNER

MONTH :

WEEK :

MONDAY

☐ _____
☐ _____
☐ _____
☐ _____

TUESDAY

☐ _____
☐ _____
☐ _____
☐ _____

WEDNESDAY

☐ _____
☐ _____
☐ _____
☐ _____

THURSDAY

☐ _____
☐ _____
☐ _____
☐ _____

FRIDAY

☐ _____
☐ _____
☐ _____
☐ _____

SATURDAY

☐ _____
☐ _____
☐ _____
☐ _____

SUNDAY

☐ _____
☐ _____
☐ _____
☐ _____

NOTE :

WEEKLY
PLANNER

MONDAY

- [ ] _____
- [ ] _____
- [ ] _____
- [ ] _____

TUESDAY

- [ ] _____
- [ ] _____
- [ ] _____
- [ ] _____

WEDNESDAY

- [ ] _____
- [ ] _____
- [ ] _____
- [ ] _____

THURSDAY

- [ ] _____
- [ ] _____
- [ ] _____
- [ ] _____

FRIDAY

- [ ] _____
- [ ] _____
- [ ] _____
- [ ] _____

SATURDAY

- [ ] _____
- [ ] _____
- [ ] _____
- [ ] _____

SUNDAY

- [ ] _____
- [ ] _____
- [ ] _____
- [ ] _____

NOTE :

WEEKLY PLANNER

MONTH :

WEEK :

MONDAY
- [ ] _____
- [ ] _____
- [ ] _____
- [ ] _____

TUESDAY
- [ ] _____
- [ ] _____
- [ ] _____
- [ ] _____

WEDNESDAY
- [ ] _____
- [ ] _____
- [ ] _____
- [ ] _____

THURSDAY
- [ ] _____
- [ ] _____
- [ ] _____
- [ ] _____

FRIDAY
- [ ] _____
- [ ] _____
- [ ] _____
- [ ] _____

SATURDAY
- [ ] _____
- [ ] _____
- [ ] _____
- [ ] _____

SUNDAY
- [ ] _____
- [ ] _____
- [ ] _____
- [ ] _____

NOTE :

List some of your accomplishments below:

Remember those fears that you wrote down earlier? Take those same fears and write them here. Now, color over them in black. Cover them so well that they no longer exist. Let this serve as a reminder of just how much God can heal you.

Letting Go

Letting go allows you to create space for growth. In this section, we will explore the art of letting go, whether it's old beliefs, toxic relationships, or self-limiting patterns. By releasing what no longer serves you, you make room for positive change and invite a sense of liberation into your life.

Activity:

Identify one thing in your life that you are ready to let go of. It could be a negative belief, a grudge, or a habit that no longer serves you. On the next page write a letter to release this from your life. Allow yourself to feel the weight lift off your shoulders and embrace the freedom that comes with letting go.

Embracing Forgiveness

Forgiveness is a powerful act of liberation and healing. In this section, we will explore forgiveness practices that will help you release resentment, anger, and pain. By embracing forgiveness, you free yourself from the emotional burdens of the past and open your heart to love, compassion, and inner peace.

Activity: Reflect on someone in your life that you are ready to forgive. Write a forgiveness letter expressing your willingness to let go of resentment. Then, if possible reach out to them and share what's on your heart. It's okay if they don't accept it. Remember, forgiveness is not about them it's about you.

Love the Lord thou God and thy neighbor as thyself. -Matt. 22:37

Forgiveness letter:

Additional space:

Additional space:

Additional space:

Additional space:

You're allowed to grow.

Change your life

Personal Growth and Empowerment

This section is dedicated to empowering you to navigate life's challenges with strength and grace. Embrace change as an opportunity for purpose, resetting your life, and uncovering your identity.

As I sit here creating this workbook, I am in the middle of a huge shift in my life. A shift from me living by other people's values and expectations to identifying and living by my own. This all hit heavy when I turned 40. It was as if I had an awakening finally getting to a place of confidence to say no. No, I don't want to be unhappy. No, I don't want to live by your rules. And no, I don't believe everything I believed growing up. I began realizing that the values I had been living by were no longer all *my* current values. They are not the things that are most important to me and how I want to live my life. Something had shifted and in the same way that no one was responsible for my happiness, no one is responsible for my inner healing, my choices or my growth.

No one can stop me.

And, no one can stop you, but you.

You previously listed five values that were most important to you. Now, list the values that you want to live by now:

Reflect on how you can live in alignment with these values and integrate them more into your daily life.

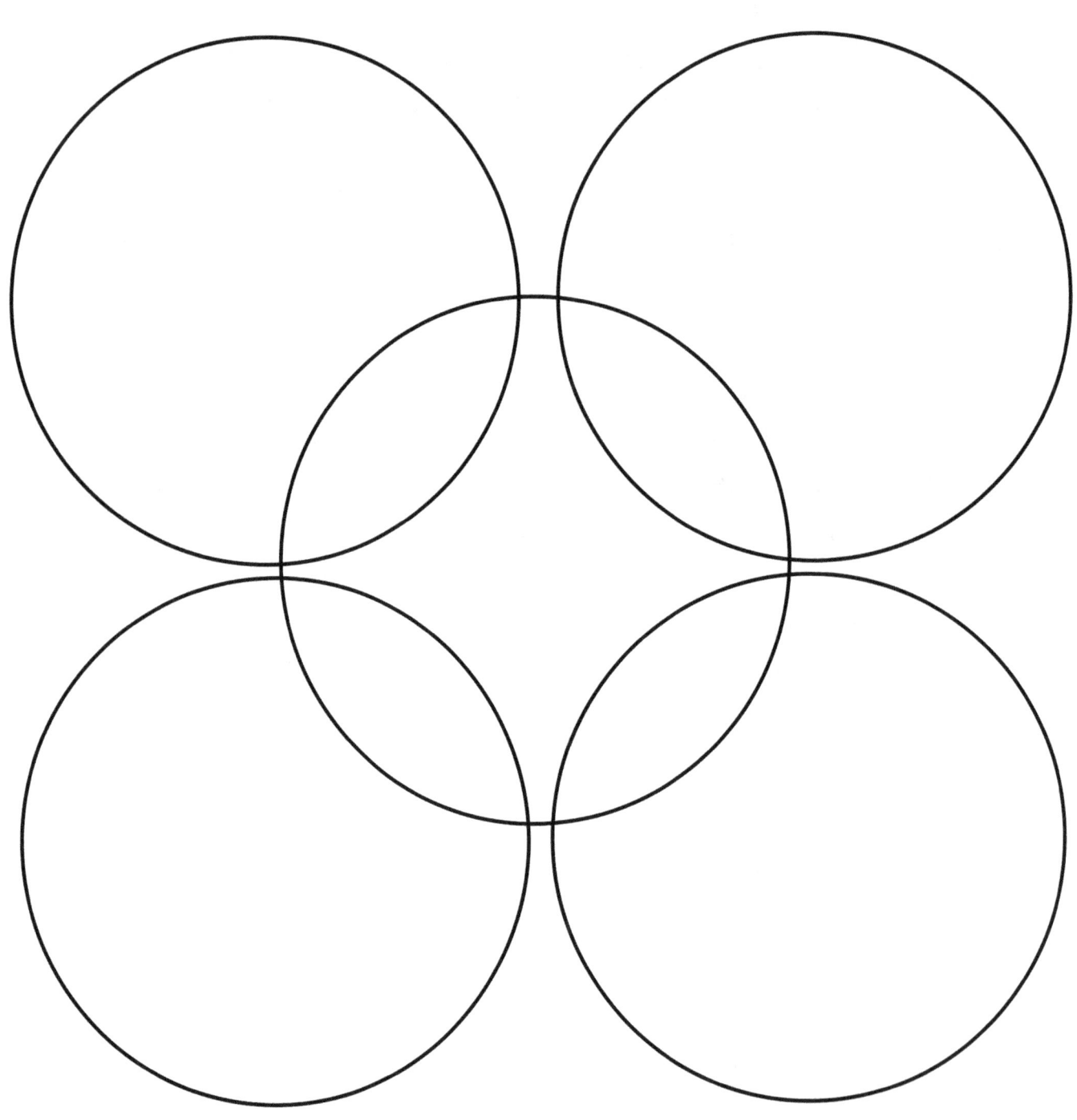

All About Me!

Facts

Favorites

Family and
Friends

Achievements

More...

How do you want to evolve?

What do you want to release? Ex. Stress, Old patterns, old relationships.

Honoring Your Needs

Setting and maintaining healthy boundaries is crucial for self-care and personal growth. By learning to honor your needs and set boundaries, you create space for self-care, assertiveness, and healthy relationships.

Activity: Take inventory of your boundaries in various areas of your life, such as work, relationships, and personal time. Reflect on where you may need to establish or reinforce boundaries. Write down three boundaries you would like to set to honor your needs and well-being.

Practice communicating these boundaries assertively and kindly, knowing that setting boundaries is an act of self-respect.

Embracing Vulnerability

Courage is the gateway to personal growth and transformation. In this section, we will explore the importance of embracing vulnerability and stepping outside of your comfort zone.

Activity: Identify an area of your life where you have been holding back or playing it safe due to fear of vulnerability. Write down three steps you can take to embrace vulnerability in this area. Challenge yourself to take those steps and embrace the discomfort that comes with vulnerability. Remember that true growth and transformation often require stepping outside of your comfort zone.

How do you define vulnerability?

When do you feel vulnerable?

When do you feel it's ok to express emotion?

Who can you be vulnerable and open with?

Identify an area of your life where you have been holding back or playing it safe due to fear of vulnerability.

Area 1

Area 2

Area 3

Area 4

space for self expression
STAY CREATIVE

Current me

Future me

Today I'm grateful for...   *Date:* _____

_____

_____

_____

_____

_____

_____

_____

_____

_____

_____

_____

_____

_____

_____

_____

_____

_____

_____

_____

_____

_____

My Vision

Health Goals

My Vision

Love Goals

My Vision

Family Goals

My Vision

Spiritual Goals

My Vision

Professional Goals

WOMAN, GO BE

Sign

Date